GW00724568

SHEARSMAN

30

30TH ANNIVERSARY — 2011

89 & 90

WINTER 2011/2012

EDITED BY
TONY FRAZER

Shearsman magazine is published in the United Kingdom by
Shearsman Books Ltd
Registered office: 43 Broomfield Road, 2nd Floor, Chelmsford,
Essex CM1 1SY *(please do not write to this address)*

New correspondence address:
50 Westons Hill Drive, Emersons Green, Bristol BS16 7DF

www. shearsman.com

ISBN 978-1-84861-155-9
ISSN 0260-8049

Acknowledgements

The poems by Yvan Goll are drawn from the 4-volume collected poems *Die Lyrik*
(Wallstein Verlag, Göttingen, 1996), ed. Barbara Glauert-Hesse. We are grateful to
Wallstein Verlag for permission to print the translations.

Subscriptions and single copies:

Current subscriptions—covering two double-issues, each around 108 pages, cost £13
in the UK, £16 for the rest of Europe (including the Republic of Ireland), and £18
for the rest of the world. Longer subscriptions may be had for a proportionately
higher payment, which insulates purchasers from further price-rises during the term
of the subscription.

Back issues from n° 63 onwards (uniform with this issue)—cost £8.50/$13.50
through retail outlets. Single copies can be ordered for £8.50, post-free, direct from
the press, through the Shearsman online store, or from bookstores in the UK and
the USA. Earlier issues, from 1 to 62, may be had for £3 each direct from the press,
where they are still available, but contact us for prices for a full, or partial, run.

Submissions

Shearsman operates a submissions-window system, whereby submissions are only
considered during the months of March and September, at which point selections
are made for the October and April issues respectively. Submissions may be sent by
mail or email, but email attachments—other than PDFs—are not accepted.
We aim to respond within 2–3 months of the window's closure.

Contents

A Splash of Red

for Anne Stevenson

For sure, with my back to the Channel—
no barn, no church for miles—this view
holds unremitting green: bracken,
unready wheat, deciduous copses,
ivy, conifers shutting off
the estuary. And vetch, dog
daisies, violets do (you're right) become
subsumed in an overall scheme.
To-day, though, a field of red
slants far off. Poppies? Too
close-set I'd say. More a chunk from Mars
dropped in defiance, hoping
to please you. Those waking at birth
in these wet, constricted islands
can't have enough of green. It helps
to forget the spreading cities,
too much mud, the trudge through slush
midwinter. That brash patch
is welcome as it's alien so, not
belonging here, gets prized. (Take those
two llamas in their Devon paddock
quietly grazing—not quite as white
as egrets flecking the Exe
into a Chinese print.) The field
in question would, were
you here, provide a hint of rubies,
life-rescuing blood, cliffs at sundown
in the Colorado desert. A boy
I was at school with confused them both—
once the golf-ball had been lofted
he couldn't find the red peg on the tee.
For him this landscape would be nothing

but tedious monochrome—unmarred
vermilion or stubborn eau-de-Nil.
You and I call the sky (all right,
at rare times) blue but can we know
we're seeing the same tint up there? What you
identify as azure may be a canopy
I see as scarlet, a real Martian treat.
For some there'll be a navy-green
or Prussian pink, their yellow-brick-roads
in purple—even lively artefacts
like ivory pimpernels, zebras
with orange stripes, cardinals
dependent on wings of silver.
Was Franz Marc's legendary world
not remarkable to him? his blue
or crimson stallions, gold-sleek
deer run-of-the-mill? I do
hope not. This poem is a gift
for you. An interrupted green, a spur
of metamorphosis, a vow
for change or instance of cold flame
to warm nostalgia at. To close
your eyes and bask in this wrong
radiance we've borrowed off that
remote, perhaps abandoned field
shifting from Parker Quink on white
to another kind of actuality.

Their Tree

She sights the tree between
two huge derelict distribution sheds.
It stops

her as if her husband
suddenly lived again.

A spring oak on the horizon –
mature with dark thick twisting limbs
holding fresh mists of greenery.

If she could remember the word,
she'd utter – *miracle*. Her children

only know trees as myths.

It's as if the tree
is balanced

      on a wire
      stretched
      between

two hollow memorials.

See how she wants so much –
wants to keep the tree.

      She puts her nearly-see-through hand
      up to the horizon, and cups the tiny oak.
      It is impossible to speak of, but
      the perfect miniature tree roots
      itself into her palm – roots through
      her veins, and feeds gently on her blood.

She & her stick-children are in awe
of the oak standing up from her hand.
The light is sprinkled on its leaves as if
green moth-dust clothed it.
And that fresh ancient scent of deep green.
Radiant green again. They weep.

Her son & daughter moan,
then yell no words. But

their breaths shake
the little oak's limbs. It sways.
And the roots, as they take
the strain and move
in her flesh,

hurt.

Now's Structures, Trossachs, January 2011

Note: *Ben Lawers* is one of the highest mountains in the Southern Highlands; its name means *hill of the loud stream*. It is near to the village of Killin, at the head of Loch Tay.

sun-wind-shine wip-sizzles soft   ly through fr   eezing air

my crampons cr   unk & chime on wind

-hardened snow-pack I'm   slung in winter's sky on

        a broad white ridge between

the snow-clothed Munros of   Beinn Glas & Ben Lawers

below Loch Tay's miles lay   as bluey-grey sky on

        snow's glossed-over lands

my crampons sh   ush-hiss through loose

gleaming snow-grains wind   lifts as smoke tr

      ails from my shins my

crampons creak on lay   ered works of wind

      wind   strea   mers of fro   zen sound   wind

layered snow-crystals cut   by motion into still   layered re

      lief maps of   layering chaos organ

ised perfectly deep-   space-blue sky

      touches white

gleaming ground hung   a   bove snow-clean glens my

      crampons grip

crink and track slippery layers my finger   tips numb as glee's zeros

sculpt my want for for   ever as (s)now

Gowl Un

I

an owl gow   n h   anged in dar   k cloud-bran

ches glow   ers a hoot of o   ther sound's sides
while wild feather-flutter fing   ers a flight's

silence claws   of solid air scritch   across a fur
ry   face light from a moon face   rotates direct

ional erot   icisms all spok   en in eye gl
int clinks cough   balls of house   -parts dissolve

in the tur   bid but moon   -illu   minated pond at
the forest's   throat the screech   of owl lung sad

ness hangs   out flapping conc   epts on a white
line of star   -stretch the mouse   in black grasses be

low itching black branches w   here two eyes &
skull-covered   feathers stare feels   a razor of breath

flip its   bones & a nest   of fluf   fy magi
cians with yolk   y ass   istants begin stripping syl

lables & dichoto   mies from a rodent's fading
skeleton last   night an   owl's soul exp   anded

and clatte   red softly across a million ferns & mosses

II

a trig   ger of gold is   touched by a light fin
ger of old bent barrel forces   a bullet's grim   ace

9

across breast-bones   gleam the hand   grabs a cold
metal organ and pumps   a life's dredge sense of

rotating   ch   amber of silent   sayings hard as
myth's disin   tegrating tipped   by skull am

bitions each slee   ping gun in the war   drobe snores
a smoke of stories   the wake   ful gun snif   fing

its way   through a soul   -parade opens
fire and in   side fire all   the heat of gods'

grief expands   in an in   stant of eyes & bone
pain is not going   to kill a gun's   aim pain the

barrel riffles as silver   scrat   ches cause a life's sp
in to craze across grief's smoo   th surface a pool

of gun-blo   od a dying   gun a crowd of frigh
tened   guns & a gun's   mother weeping gold &

sold (golden souled) bull   ets down steel cheeks

III

an owl-gown   hanged in a trigger of gold dark
cloud branches   glower touched by a light
finger a hot of other sounds   on old bent barrel

forces sides while wild feather bullets a grimace
across flut   ter-fingers a flight's breast-bone
gleam the hand grabs   a cold silence claws   of

solid air sc   ritch across a metal organ furry face
light from a life's   dr   edge a moon   face
rotates a rotating   chamber dire   ctional erotic

isms all silent saying hard spoken   in eye
glint clinks myths   disintegrate cough balls
of house   parts tipped by skull   ambitions' each

sleeping gun   dissolves in the turbid but moon
-illuminated pond at the wardrobe snore   by fo
rest's   throat the smoke   of stories wakeful

      gun sniffing screech   owl lung

sadness way through a soul-parade hangs out   fl
apping concepts opens   fire   & inside fire on wh
ite line of star   stretch the mouse in all   the heat

of gods the black grass   below grief expands itching
black branches were instants   of eyes & bone two
eyes & skull covered pain not going   to kill a gun's

aim feather stares   feel   a razor the barrel   riffles
as silver breaths flip bone   a nest of magician's
scratches cause a life with yolky   assistants begin

spin to   craze across stripping syllables   & grief's
smooth surface a pool of gun   blood & dichotomies
from a rodent's last   night a dying   gun a crowd

a fad()ing   skeleton and owl's soul expanded off
frightened   guns a gun's mother wee   ping gold
clattered softly across a million   ferns & mosses &

      sold bul   lets down st   eel cheeks

Count down

9.

when underfoot the dust won't
rest where it fell as the ground
trembles becoming nothing
less than itself at each step
down in time out of joint time
being all we have to hold
us together I listen
to the empty corridors
like a skull that could sing once

8.

when a song with no body
but clearly belonging to
someone else keeps returning
what obligations do I
have to the shadows that fall
between the buildings between
a thought and a word between
a word and a tongue moving
across the dust and ashes

7.

when dust keeps returning in
particles of what used to
be solid ground over which
no-one flies any more there
are steps descending into
deep industrial echoes

of what was swept clean away
where the earth has never stopped
falling back in blind faces

6.

when blindness is all that makes
the next step possible in
counting down deeper further
under the dust is music
each word a furious ghost
of its own future descent
descant to scored line out of
time I'm out of time again
here help me please count me in

5.

when I count myself among
crowds in reverberant space
as voices collide with walls
falling through the missed letters
on someone else's tongue I
return as dust as if dust
is an echo as if an
echo is the depth of a
word deserted by a mouth

4.

when the desert whipped into
wind falls as dust covering
skin with finest particles
settling in red who can say
where nomad journeys begin

or solid ground ends in rose
haze on a windscreen distance
diminishes in lost scales
blurred in azure unmeasured

3.

when distances are measured
in days between skin that will
by then have been shed lightly
in particles of dust no
protection against the loss
that's a fact grating against
skin's definition of what
I'd like to think it bounded
against the harm of speaking

2.

when harm is shed lightly as
garments that fall from skin shed
at the centre of dust I
am distracted particles
in all directions cinders
scatter at a moment's edge
the skeleton of a thought
call it life in the stillness
underneath the churning earth

1.

when there's no stillness in thought
or in earth that is scattered
finely on every surface
looking back at you from a
future nobody can see

where is the way down and how
many steps must be counted
as the scored earth turns over
underfoot where dust won't rest

from The Rooms

Room 321

When entering the room you're in the same
place yet again as other rooms forget
themselves
                    repeating the distance from door
to bed
         chair to window
                    window to floor
to mirror

              Here you are overcome by
your love of mirrors as the slow movement
underneath the surface becomes your skin

In the force field of possible lives you
are taking three steps to the centre of
the stained carpet

              It's here that everything
is happening twice
                once in the body
and once in the words for it
                   and there's no
escaping that song in your head
                   the one
that was in the room and is now in you

Elizabeth Robinson

No One Knew Who Lee Miller Was

At an early age, I broke open my very self and let

no one tell you that it was otherwise. A violation

subverts itself, becomes a camera: I was never,

not ever,

afraid of controlling light.

*

Slightly before dawn

the light bounce off my flesh. This curious

source preceded and provoked

the day that was to come, but which had not

yet shed anticipation

of the sun.

Wrongly, the eye

considers itself a lens, and, wrongly, sight

is thought to redound

to its organ.

*

The body, I can give evidence, is an instrument of

sensitivity. It can learn; it

can absorb its own records.

*

At an early age, I saw all that I need see,

any yet the eye flushes itself out,

not with tears, not with its evidentiary

but with a form of trust

that goads it forward

to the next excess.

Evelyn Nesbitt and Stanford White taking a bow at the Madison Square Garden Rooftop Theatre

This is our final performance as scholars of the structures

of intimacy

The velvet swing lurches forward, secured overhead only

by the chalk of the sky.

Passenger, alight.

Architects are scientists of beauty. Lovers
prove fidelity by betraying their own

purities.

Applause, like the report of gunshot, stains us all.

Winston Churchill & Crockett Johnson (authorof Harold and the Purple Crayon) meet at last

Great men observe the making and unmaking of the world.
Fanciful illustrations an bon mots
are theirs to claim,
to coin, to mint as
currency while
bombs
drop.

And the greater protagonsits
are not men, nor
even real.
      This is our bald fact.

Theirs is to draw in the actual as if it
were a refugee in flight.
To reverse gravity as in a cartoon where
bombs bounce, coins
buy pie, and the character
we claim as our own, bona fide, draws up the covers,
draws up a treaty, never
calls it a draw, this
purple cartoon of the real.

ANDY BROWN

Jeroen van Aken

It's 1516. My sixty-third year
in Hertogenbosch, this cloth and iron town
remote from the heart in Northern Brabant.

My wife and I live out our final days
in a world full of infidelity,
laid low by sin. For ten years I've painted

nothing, though I've seen our churches burning,
flaming river banks, villages on fire,
towers toppling here and there through thin ice,

Hell erupting from underground, each rock
pierced by trees—trees lifting up rocks—dark eyes
and ears listening from under a stone.

I am as a stranger in my own time:
like a dried-up riverbed that runs through
a deeply fissured land, its recessed crags

steep above the mild plains, then out beyond,
along the desolate coast where tall ships
smoulder and go down in the curving bay;

or closer still where birds of day chase off
the predators of night who roost inside
the hollows of a giant human tree.

The crescent moon of unbelief hangs high,
a glint in the night, like the eyes of owls,
of magpies or of swans, or moist-eyed toads . . .

and though the peaceful Lowlands lie around,
corruption spreads as far as men can see.
The world cares nothing for one man's torments—

this morning in the street where charlatans
make livings fooling lords and fine ladies
with conjuring and hocus-pocus, where

beggars and cripples scrape the dust for coins,
I watched a dupe refill his leaky jug
at the village pump: he cranked the handle,

water flowed, his pots drank every drop,
and yet the level never rose for all
the cracks that crazed the bottom of his flask.

We are actors in our own dumb routines;
gullible peasants in makeshift shelters,
vagabonds sleeping at doorways to caves,

wanderers in temporary dwellings.
A man crawls into a beehive in vain
hoping to find rest. Frail children set out

to sail their scuppered boats upon the stream
and drown. What threatens us, we made ourselves.
The end is imminent—terrors close in—

so why do they refuse to mend their ways?
The fortunes and misfortunes of a man
reach past memory and presentiment.

As when the inconceivable bursts through
the surface of our lives—when the inside
becomes outside—so all is upside down.

The burghers are fools, concerning themselves
in sensual pleasures and frivolity,
black witchcraft, devilry and alchemy.

They dance a zigzag path through the public
spectacle, forgetting it was a clown
who last died on the gallows, on the wheel.

How did the pantomime of skeletons
in cages come to be so trivial?
The uniform of folly's worn by all.

It is 1516. Righteousness fights
with temptation; punishment with reward.
Turn away from the things of the world. Turn

back to Time's passage to eternity.
Hold fast in hand your pilgrim's cockleshell.
Hold fast still, Brethren of the Free Spirit.

Chimeras

A cyborg is a cybernetic organism, a hybrid of machine and
organism . . . The cyborg is a creature in a post-gender world.
        —Donna Harraway, *A Cyborg Manifesto*

Apple-shaped women (triangle downward)
have broader shoulders compared to their hips;
compared to their levers, their pulleys and tackle.
Apple-shaped women have rounded machines
with multiple cannons, completed in copper,
mounted on wheels of turtle design,
powered by enormous treadmills, steam,
or horses. Apple-shaped women have slim
legs and thighs. Their bellies and chests
can seem out of proportion. Fat is mainly
spread across the tummy, face and bust.

> The *ectomorph* is small framed and thin
> with narrow shoulders, hips and slots

to view the enemy. He may have trouble
gaining weight; he may have a *ballista*
with several springs, a level bar, a cog.
The ectomorph has trouble building
muscle, a braking system, or solid shields
of wooden planks. An ectomorph needs
to eat as much carbohydrate as he can
to become a one-man battleship, or rocket-
powered cannon-ball that flies ten thousand feet.

Banana (or rectangular) women have waists
nine inches smaller than the hips or bust.
Banana-shaped women are rotated by screws,
sail-powered tanks, by spikes and pitons.
The wheel-lock systems and scaling ladders
of banana-shaped women have scythes
joined to their chariots at the rear. The body fat
of banana-shaped women is spread around
the abdomen, buttocks, chest and face.
This creates the typical ruler. Their shells,
filled with gunpowder, explode upon impact.

The *mesomorph* is normal weight: neither
fat nor skinny. He packs on muscle easily,
stands angled to absorb the force of recoil
with his system of gears attached to driving
wheels. He can lose weight easily, is more
than just a shell, with room enough for a man
to sit inside and aim his mid-range barrel.
He has shoulders wider than his hips;
breech-loading cannons arranged around
the rim of his wheels. As they rotate
he arches and discharges each radial bow.

Pear or bell-shaped women (triangle up)
have hips much wider than their busts.
Fat distribution varies, with fat tending
to deposit in the buttocks, hips, and thighs.

Women of this type tend to have a (relatively)
large rear, robust thighs, a small(er) bosom,
flexible arms bent back with ropes or a winder
mechanism to power the penetrating effects
of missiles hurled against the city walls.
Body fat is spread around the waist, the upper
abdomen and underneath the armoured plates.

> The *endomorph* is considered to be
> pear shaped. Meaning his hips are wider
> than his shoulders; meaning by striking a pin,
> by turning a winch, or pulling on a rope
> he can gain weight easily and is curvy;
> meaning that he is cast in iron or bronze
> and that his cranks attached to trundle wheels
> allow him to sling a grappling hook across
> the walls. An endomorph should eat less
> carbohydrates. An endomorph has four scythes
> attached to his machine, like helicopter blades.

Hourglass women (triangles opposing,
facing in) have hips and busts of (almost)
equal size, with narrow waists, bridges
and battering rams. Their body fat is spread
around both upper and lower abdomen.
This body type enlarges arms, chest, hips,
before the waist, which sits built into
a brazier of coals. When their water turns
to steam, it drives a rack of fourteen guns
arranged in tiers, striking them with hammers
from two remote-control firing mechanisms.

Note: Bosch's paintings abound with hybrid bodies: half-human, half-machine. Accordingly, the poem is a chimera of two texts: a description of the war machines invented by Leonardo da Vinci in Bosch's era, and a present-day guide to body types.

MARIANNE BURTON

The Shoes

She found or bought them at a stall she said.
But I say a soldier gave them to her.

Took them off a woman who lay dead.
Perhaps the dying happened a tad quicker

for his help. Who knows the truth. But I know
she wore those shoes. Their stilted heels

the grotesque probosci of giant insects,
their leather outers smooth as slipped calf,

their colour the scarlet of fresh-flayed meat.
Most comfortable in the region, she claimed.

And she was probably right. But I know
after a time with every step they held her

closer, hugged her tighter, burnt her rawer,
buried in her deeper, until her feet

started to slip, the damp started to slide,
moist to wet to wetter as though her feet's

sweat were pouring into a salt wrap,
as though her flesh were liquefying.

When she peeled them off, her skin was red
with blood. But it was the shoes were bleeding.

She tried to lose them, shake herself free,
she tried to throw them away, but her hands

stuck fast, the felt liners clung to her fingers.
She reeled along the track, her heels toes soles

stung and dusty, blistered and mauve, in her hand
the shoes which bled every step of the road.

2am : Night Feed

My blue-skinned parasite, my warm-lipped fish,
dovetailing back to being the one body
we once were, snug-fitting—the other joinder,
not lovers, but lovers, my breast, your mouth,
the suckle rhythm of the two-beat blood,
heart flow of pull and swallow,
churn and curd, protein and serotonin.

My co-conspirator. Your meninges throb
through your fontanelle as we drift towards
the deep sea sleep of the calved whale
and all the other mammals in your brother's book,
the ewe, the ox, the lemur, the manatee,
kinkajou, chevrotain, cloud leopard,
kangaroo, pronghorn, elephant shrew,

ROSS HAIR

Turan

the rose is
the trope

the flower
Eros holds

from A Round Portchester, *A Calendar*

spring
again

Proserpina

"sharp
in the grass"
& grain

§

fall boughs
seed green –
autumn's testa
like Buddha's
in Gloucester
harbour
the Padma

§

restless summer
– sheen –
fidget of light

on leaf

wax effervesce
flourish, flare
green

still vermilion winter
pools mizzle light –

dusk spread
senses damped,
dim into night

Static in Winter

They dig & seek what they cannot corner
                              or gather
a barricade of gloves carried abottom
this staircase slipped with ice

first leaves & now snow
                              scraped off & thrown
to the side to exchange scrunch for slick

They pivot & catch what they're compelled to release
no further down without a point
                                        to press
displace   move air to ice

air to grind & erase   disappear
what for now occupies air's space

They flock & bother what they cannot flee
the water stuck in its throne   listing
as if solid it must be   float or floe

on the river river road   moving
road   moving river   road

They rock & shutter what they feel must cease
some sliver of water dangling fine
                              no drip
some sliver to impress on the ground its need

to rise above itself itself & carry what has no desire
to go

They fathom & totter what they face down in toto
                                        or intact
a minor movement & series
                              a flagrancy of fact
no sooner or later than nothing or now

the sound a drift   a sullied bespect
the lens a fracture of light & despond

They shriek & shimmy what they feel obliged to borrow
as a friend will remove & never return
the lack a ring that grows over time

a word skirts   stalls the matter
a final celestial sidewalk strummed choir

I borrow your brother & blink all atangent
my stickerish limbs know the price of a fall
no parting or such fielding these questions

the ice when it melts will right what is sinking
a torn apart bargain for any still standing

I wring & deform that which is lodged
hand a cradle for anything swollen
oh please don't befriend or relieve me

this freeze-shattered fact a matter of ache
buried until plain speech won't arouse it

I shake & I shake   the liquid now streaming
a full-headed fright the road is all closed
no lanterns or godsends to burrow me forward

sheets & drifts guide the discarded
a foreseen insensate puddled beneath me

The wheels of the burden a curtain of precip
no sight emerges to cull the collected
the snow   do you see it   it covers

itself a snow-covered font
the blend is what in the end fills us

This they I posit   this you   some we
what I to deliver or beg for inspect
when all I require is an hour for slumber

a pillow of wet   a blanket of ice
a surface still & unchanging

Come   someone says   loudly & with gust
we huddle   this I   a snow-stricken force
come   someone says   & we collect as if pulled

a shore-twisted alabast minus the rust
some gargle of bodies   this topple of us

Come someone says   they will be here
                              in breath
a backward entice to shriek us all forward
come someone says   we the sore-appled

a dimness is arcing its falling in our direction
a stillness of ice   a performance unfrozen

The view we are left with   a silicon vision
the words & their colors all undressed in the cold
everything soon will be numbered   yawned open

unless the illusion of movement reclaims its divide
decreases our sorrows   you static   you snow

Jaime Robles

"Utere felix, domina Juliane"
—Inscription on a gold bracelet, Hoxne treasure, c. A.D. 400

A hand thrust through the circle
of space drawn by a hoop of yellow gold,
telling of blood and bone
in the center of nothingness

•

The bracelet in turn wraps to the wrist,
garlands her skin
with leaves, doorways

•

Her bracelet slips up and drops
as her arm rises and falls.
A hand's width holds it to the wrist.
Glimmer anchors it in the eye of an onlooker.

•

Who is to say words are without attraction:
WEAR THIS WITH JOY, LADY JULIANA

•

Gold circles endlessly,
and part of the world drops out again:
the penetration of cold
empty sky
gleam of the stream's thin casing over stone's surface
the thick paste of silt
all furrowing round paths

"Utere felix, domina Juliane"
—Inscription on a gold bracelet

Because he sees her as beautiful
he is pulled to the side
not joined but trapped in her gravity,
unbuttoning his momentum

•

Though beauty unconsidered
seems like light or distance
in relief: a flight

•

The sway would fall
magnetically inscribing a caress
across her thigh-inward spills,
an unhealed bifurcation

•

There is no symmetry here even though
bracelets encircle both wrists

•

Smooth surfaces form an ecosystem:
Her mouth like the forest floor is humid
indivisible, yes, teeming
The tongue's movement more than muscular-
requiring a parade of vowels;
she pulls back the hair from her forehead
revealing a frame of white froth

Matching Gold Bangles

I

Clay clasping the wrist, thumb and finger: manacled, mute.
The tongue a basket-forest of gold corrugate: scuddering
cries, muffled, fallen reeds: plaid of stalks. Speech stopped
at the first gate; in the background, disaster: a procession of doors,
each closed, each to be opened. Pushed rustling into the earth,
wrapped, the horizon a whirlpool. The soft shush of breath and heart's
outward flight quelled, fallen earthward turning-slowly,
sound withdrawn. Indwelling the coat of flesh the muscle of tongue

---

      clasping   wrist, thumb and finger:

                          the circumference of forest.

leaves mute
           —gold: *chuddering*

                    Speech contracts

        rustling

---

corrugate

speech

nets the soft breath

wresting

flesh

2

Fixing a bond, crushing the hand: slipped over. Thoughts—
urges-packed in fabric: press of soft mouth against careful mouth,
short cropped grass stifled, branch dappled. Prized bits and pieces
nested into each other; in the foreground, sentences: encircling gold
lacing matter and sound, layered like onions, rattling up from the earth;
wrapped, the perimeter of the wrist. Clink. Click. Clatter. The past's
forward flight looking back, always, turning often and again-reluctantly,
folded, replaced, altered. Indwelling the rod of bone the shatter of tooth

---

                    a hand slips

                              across

                                        his soft mouth

lacing reluctant matter and sound

                                        —circle of gold

bits and pieces

clatter

Rupert M. Loydell

Soap

I like the way this soap I've just opened
has SOAP stamped on it. Bad science fiction
has info dumps to explain to the reader
how worlds work; onscreen that means
signs everywhere. Why doesn't the sky
have SKY written on it in the clouds?
Why doesn't the wall have THIS WAY UP
in contrasting bricks? If I was dyslexic
words might appear broken up, interrupted
by globes of light. Since I'm not it doesn't
and I know the names of most things I use.
It's good to know that soap is soap and
words is words, at least most of the time.

Lost Property
for Nathan

'He looks like lost property now'
  —Craig Raine, 'The Tattooed Man'

Bill was asking what my new paintings were about
and I facetiously said 'paint'. But as you observed,
just when you think you are talking about one thing
it turns out to be a conversation about something else.

One moment it's a discussion about poetry,
the next it's the mystical meaning of your name
if you translate it into numbers according to
an Aramaic scroll recently discovered by a lake.

Then it turned out to be Peter's round and
as he made the trip to the bar the talk moved on

to yesterday's television that we hadn't watched
anyway and films none of us will ever see.

I was doing my best to keep up and so were you
but it all went into a spin. Art is art and talk
is talk but if no-one knows where it is leading
then all that's left is luggage on the floor,

full of our frustration. Anyway, what a time
it's been. I've still not thanked you for the drink,
am still wondering how important it is
that the letters in your name add up to seven.

An End to Worrying

'People said it was the future then, and we
liked falling into mirrors'
            —Matthew Zapruder, 'Poem (for Grace Paley)'

The boat was as dry as dry could be
although the awning was full of holes
which hadn't let rainwater in.
I wondered how this could be
as the tide slowly covered the mud,
as the wind rose and blew me
into tomorrow, which was only
a reflection of today, still populated
by the exactly the same people.

The poem was as poetic as could be
expected but your theory is full of holes
which leave the reader adrift and lead
to bad reviews. It is hard to turn back
the tide and reinvent the wheel.
Soundbites and metaphors, similes
and asides all converge in your poems,
which you say are something to do
with truth and self-expression.

It's a bit like the ghost of tomorrow
walking into the room, a bit like
the past has happened before. The past
has happened before. I don't want to
alarm you but this rings too many bells
and I am trying to warn you, to scare
you into moving somewhere else where
there is a waterproof waterproof cover
and everyone is their own true self.

The future is as uncertain as could be
although it will probably be alright
in its own peculiar way. It is just
time passing, and the memory of things
affecting me this way, just my way
of passing the time. It is that time
of year again; soon it will all be over,
soon it will again be spring. It will take
ages to dry out, I shouldn't wonder,

forever to undo. It is the little things
that get me down, not the grand theory
of space & time, or even the price
of drinks. The same people always
seem the same to me, and the ones
we want to see live far too far away.
Everything is not connected, there is
no true sequence of lies. Tomorrow
I will try to put an end to worrying.

Tati the Parrot

The Polymath is creating a model to demonstrate analogies of space and time across physical and biological structures. He nurtures it in his head and in the diagrams he draws with coloured pens—calculations a cosmologist transfers into Euclidian graphics. Meanwhile the Art Dealer is asking him questions about Pythagoras and the pattern of 3 in the rosette windows of Milan Cathedral adding that 52 is the number he found in a book about the Dome of the Rock in Jerusalem where a medieval Arab traveller witnessed liturgy occurring. Today and every day at the appointed hour 52 lascars anoint the tip of the Rock with sweet-smelling ointments. And because his hotel window looks down on a second-hand bookshop in Zurich he slips out and buys *Tales of Tati the Parrot* who whispers, in attentive ears only, 52 moral/behavioural injunctions. I say it must be the same parrot that flew into John Ashbery's *L'Heure Exquise*. Then he tells us that a medieval numerologist may for a fee like 3 hens eggs or a bushel of barley inform you that the number 5, compounded with a Pythagorean triangle, mutates into the Octagon which supports the Dome of the Heavens.

Codes & Folios

The Art Dealer is collecting citations from the most ancient texts—the *Dead Sea Scrolls* and the *Codex Sinaiticus*: the solar and lunar week, lunations and weekday dates, monthly and yearly cycles from Babylonia and Egypt which the ancients used as mnemo-technique to teach computation of reliable religious festivals. The folios are stretched skin of donkey or antelope and it's thought 360 animals were slaughtered for the *Codex*. He's trawling for Jewish and Christian references before turning to the Arabic sources. He has produced eighteen Word pages—about six thousand words itching in his fingertips. Outside of this writing process he's forever 'losing marbles', as though his brain-box had shifted to another zone throwing an entirely new and stretched perspective on the world.

Geometries & Numbers

I

The Polymath is sitting at the white round table drawing tangents with his protractor, set-square, ruler and compass. The Art Dealer hovers by hoping against hope that the proportional measurements between the 'dots' on his bronze Insignia, a stylised representation of a symmetric 8-petal flower, match those of the Rosette in Milan Cathedral. As for me, I'm struggling with my *terza rima*, slightly abashed to be using Dante's template for a work originating in Arabic and, albeit *pre*-Islamic, nothing to do with the Trinity. To compound matters I'm dealing with eight stanzas per page and five pages per canto. I redeem myself by thinking of 'Lalla Maghnia'. At least she is in sonnets, thus the whole work is in multiples of seven.

II

The wall is covered in chalk equations, diagrams and formulae. I'm planning to paper another with his beautiful pen & ink diagrams. He frequently achieves an almost complete model but there's always one essential component that refuses to fit and I tell him it's like doing the Rubik's Cube. On a dresser next to the old Dutch wood-burner there's a wooden ship he brought me from a tea plantation in Java. We seldom drink tea in Spyglass Inn and when we dance on the boards and hear a thud everyone cries *There goes the ship!* Yes, a frieze of bright-inked diamonds, cubes, rectangles and triangles and from the ceiling octahedra and tetrahedra flying around like Chinese kites.

My Theory of Relativity

It's been three years since I moved onto a street
made of real shoe-polished cobblestones.

You walked on them when you visited that first December.
I still can't walk in heels without tripping.

People laugh and think that I'm drunk. And I do drink
when it's sunny or really gloomy, the sky

like wet cigarette smoke. I've also lightened my hair—
a lot.
                    If you lived in a flat just up the road

and I'd come round last year (when I wasn't feeling like myself)
for low fat biscotti, your weird metaphors and intangible

advice and you'd told me that terrible thing,
would I have told you that it was just the cocaine?

Probably not. I would have cried, comfort-eaten spaghetti
and avoided you for months. Now when I see you

from my window, walking down the cobbled street,
I still feel more than three thousand miles of guilt.

Secret Family Recipe

Inside the room of fine china
there's the smell of pickled onion.
Flour the paper walls. Toss the greens

in the clear glass. My hands
are wooden up to the elbow.
Fingers stiff and slick with oil.

The glasses keep breaking, I say.
The crystal rain falls into the deep
ceramic sea. The whole room

smells of seahorses,
of whales, of starfish.
Or is it just salmon again?

I'll peel the scales off the sizzling pan
and throw them back
into the foam.

You are some of the few
who know my ancestry.
Time has split my tail and my toes

have torn their webs. Only you
around this table know of my scales,
my lust for salt and excessive thirst.

Look at my shins, my secret
lineage. I pan fry my family.
Blood lines of Omega3.

The threads of white bone,
followed by green leaves,
peeled roots and oil.

Pod

O night who doth entreat thee . . .

A road contiguous to heath land:
brushwood & teasel   spawn-weed & weasel
. . . from which do stars appear
(She) enquires of the nature   inveigles
directions   describes the environ
in the manner of one who lingers
on detail – the precision
of stone   the fey semblance
of shadow

What may it be?

~

The tarmac track:
Inquisitive folk along the way
mud-patch & cross-ditch   pitch-axe & foible
fob-witch yarn-catch bale-switch   dabble
a lowered brow   a beggared land
outreached – those rags
have seen   wondrous days
rat-a-tat   worry-snatch   grass-talk   twiddle

~

A manner of placing:

One (who) speaks out

quibble-tip   tease-trim   jest-quip   venture
left-brim   nestle-brain   mind-meld   mortar

seems to know her   So

repeats her question

underlined   & without malice

Arrives at a halt

A thing approaches – maybe a donkey

Here and there are finders

verge-bare   scavenge-heap   scrip-scree   debris

~

A lot happens:

(She) is allotted the task of sweeping up

twinkle little eye (well met)
mirth & mire   sweet & sly   scour the sky   hither & by

without

her cardigan – fine points

maketh the difference – her hair

united in chains of colour

~

O'er the brink of a hillock:

A little picture

calendar – tiny days

and months dangle

~

Corollary:

Through night doth she wonder . . .
pea-case hornet-husk shell-pare sliver

(She) boils beetroot sweet red beetroot

buries bulbs bidding

their little shoots

Progress

Were I   to be tamed   sufficed

by the odd mention   the occasional

wisp in the cornea − the perfect place

for an image − though solitary

& unknowing   well then

thy bespoke − nay − homemade

life as I   would describe

may flail − a somnambulist's

portion   though do not let it

flounder

Tim Allen

Four Poems from *Default Soul*

noise escapes from ever quiet air race
first we'll miss you then we'll miss ourselves
the flowers walk their narrative founders
multicultural children rheumatoid eagles

dunes left in the dune crèche all day
guidebook head spends all day on the tram
my work colleagues have crystallised
ecstasies of old rebellion untroubled

mysteries of ancient summer train sets
little trotty wagtail nails the performance
the paradox train tangent arid thermal
European climbs lake

a method acting burglar is most dangerous
bulky non-stick slender nonsense sticks
if it's going to happen let it ice-age
it's a risk but it makes sense

don't try to sleep in contradictory focus
take some advice stick to the story
spray a spray of moonlight on a spray of starlit flowers
learning a new language this late is folly

the cliff absorbs all the cliff walks
the cliff absolves all kisses and caresses
get down on your flickery knees like a cliff
put the sea back where you found it

book table is a gravity free environment
lighthouse keeper's cat automatically sick
cabin cruiser catalogue for casual excess
licks up murdered mystery shopper

ape above western porch mimics the east
flash roads lag behind good girl in new city
a magazine left open like a gaping abyss
church porch quite possible without a church

hygienic fellow traveller carries on unveiling
new city humpty dumps into empty test-tube
come down from the mountain full of yourself
spectral electrician in damp heaven

there are no trees in wonderland
i wonder why there are no trees there
there are no nests for the birds in the trees
i wonder why there are no nests there

ironing a union jack under glass miles
nymph behaving just like a businessman
sheathed landscape adoption agency
naked river flows raincoat over arm

the relay baton is rusty so's the runner
that shimmer is the shine of a deep doom
a quick blast of harmless schizophrenia looms
underarm queuing in cratered sky

Intertextuality

```
It's always at the edge
of things you
know that bit in between or this
     that bit in between
as wild blue
in a field of lemon
the call of a bird
somewhere that chill
a shock of berry
  a cosmic shard
something that shudders
and departs
at the edge of the eye
far off
```

```
Let's call to arms repetition
seagull hearts rise and
                   Tall
faltering loves timidity
rises on the blue horizon
drifting fragments of gold
tiny fragments of tranquility
moondust floats in the breeze
was it just one small step
untested experimental
new
```

We always come to this
point of destruction word
smith instigator of the inane
    would it be that nothing remained
    One day after the other

 follow me
    along
this
    forest floor by this river
     foot

    fall loose
      root indefinite
           fault line

Listen! Listen!
Can you hear it feel it
    Gathering in the half light
marvelling in the fauna
nuance as a grappling
condition as a cycle

Listen can you hear it
in all these fettered emotions
conclusions
    acting snap
  reality

          convolute and unquantifiable
      i see it in every scent
        as the serenity that dies
          on an impulse
          on every flower here
here

      and

                  here

          imaginas in the woods
          too much congested
          the light catches   way
          the eye

          are there too many
          ...intangibles
          just be simply

GEORGE MESSO

Aligned Underfoot

In those days, your best poems
lived under bridges, in wild garlic;

tiny constellations dreaming out
from lost rings of darkness. Well,

there must have been other things too.
There were: flowers —small & white—

but precisely who was reading
that *Book of Brilliance*, I don't know.

Go back a little, I missed something
—it's all shade but there is a place

darker, deeper than the rest, where
earth is always bare, perpetually dry,

where nothing grows, nothing could,
a perfect *where* to hide: your enemies,

yourself, a treasure.

The Chart Room of Abu Bashaar

Before the sun is even up
forests are on the move.

Sailing through milk fat pasture,
there is a scraping of bark,

a scoring of hulls on hobbled earth.
And from where I'm at

I'm willing to consider their pine flotilla
a refuge for my long self-pity.

Down the valley we go! Let's drink
from the tears of crushed leaves,

anoint our brows with globes of sap.
Set each man to his mast

and each branch to its purpose.
Can there really be a thing more extraordinary

than the terrible rib-cracking roar
of a valley clearing its throat?

Lay down our position, Master Lee,
twenty degrees to the east

where already the climbing dial
illumines our edge and end.

Into whatever abyss it rises from
we throw ourselves like tinder

into a furnace. Each man to his mast!
And me to my self-pity.

Envy

He's nothing to me the attractive man
Listening in Tuscany to one mandolin
The light chartreuse beyond the window
Whose arch is high whose sill is low

Listening in Tuscany to one mandolin
Dark-red cravat and sweet-oiled hair
Whose arch is high whose sill is low
One of two men at the luncheon party

Dark-red cravat and sweet-oiled hair
And two girls their eyes reposed into
One of two men at the luncheon party
Youthfulness a square white tablecloth

And two girls their eyes reposed into
orbital ridges shadowed pink and yellow
Youthfulness a square white tablecloth
Connecting to the luck of ripe plums

Orbital ridges shadowed pink and yellow
The light chartreuse beyond the window
Connecting to the luck of ripe plums
He's nothing to me the attractive man

Muse of the Rocks

"Why don't you just swim the whole length of it on
A deep stored breath, you swimming champeen?" so yelled
The Animus of the Precipice from on

High. "Faster! Faster!" But what good is that? I
Want to stroke, not faster, but smoother, you dumb
Son of a bitch. "There! Over there!" Wha'? but I

Am swimming, can barely hear. "Bird! Eyeing your
Pretty red-seaweed hair for his mate! Wait, it's
A female bird of prey, rust yearly, so you're

In luck, she's my neighbor! Little-Redtail-Hawk!"
Well, if my hair's for *her* nest, not his, then fine.
"It's okay!" I shout to Old-Man-Mountain-Hawk

When next my head comes up. Now I'm Εὐρώπη.
This is a Lake where a meteorite struck.
The Ledge says, "There are no outlets in Europe

For the kind of hairdryer you're used to, let
Alone the flatiron. You'll simply have to use
The Sad Iron, or let it frizz, let it frizz, let

Go." I see Eliot in the Alps, yellow
Kneesocks in rhythm to his climb up up and
His calves like a butterfly all in yellow.

Cin-de-rell-a dressed in yellah went upstairs
To kiss her fellah how many kisses did
He get?" 1 2 3 "and she's buy... ing... the... stair...

Way..... t'heavennnn" Led Zeppelin the last time
They sing it, slowwwed dowwn. Fare thee well, 4/4 time.

Maledictions

May you marry somebody twice your age.

May you marry somebody half your age.

May you feel decay in every one of your corpuscles.

May you believe that your needles have eyes when in fact those have been filled in with superglue and the glue has become not translucent but transparent and you will think you are losing your own eyesight every time you go to tighten up a sagging button.

Laundry. Seriously.

Heathcliff! Heeeeathcliiif! Heeeeeeeeath Cliiiiiiiiiiiiiiiiiiiif!

May every contest you enter be won by a guy who writes with acute nostalgia for his past as if it were the past.

May you get a job as an upholsterer in Hell and use sunscreen without noticing its use-by date had come and gone and win on a game show a gimongous SUV with a four-cylinder engine.

May pulling apart the two halves of the split ends of your long winter-dry hair be your best hobby ever.

Anthony Caleshu

from The Victor Poems

The Pleasure and Utility of Friendship

Friendship, Victor, is almost analogous to living.
But, so too is taxidermy almost analogous to living.
We watch the twitching squirrels, the shifting moles, the fox ferrying by.
None are yet dead, not even us.
Who was it that risked death for justice?
We once found you with meningitis, curled up like a mouse on the floor.
We all peed orange for a week.
Bah to death! we said, pushing past the nurse to see you.
Bah to death! we say sliding over the ice to see you now.
Doubt, like fear, is a trait best captured in the cold.
The snow is falling into our eyes—captured!
Our love of you and your love of us, returned—captured!
Nobody, but nobody Victor, would choose to live without friends.
Why do you choose to live without friends?—captured!
We would share with you the last segment of our last orange, the size
      of a lime.
Our footsteps haven't been returned in the longest time . . .
Our friendship is private, voluntary, and forever happening in the
      distance.
Our friendship is taxidermic.
We imagine the fox with the squirrel, stuffed, in a dioramic game of cards.
The fox loses his shirt, his clothes, the feelings in his toes, whilst the
      squirrel stays warm in a second pair of socks.
'What if I need the second pair of socks? What if my own toes get
      cold?'
The friendship of animals is one of utility.

Where our friendship, Victor, is one of pleasure... the pleasure, say,
      of a pair of seal-fur lined gloves.
We've never asked you for anything, Victor, we just always assumed.
And, O, how our hands are cold, Victor! O how our hands are so cold!

Nothing Has Ever Been Achieved without Enthusiasm

Victor, what can we say?
Forgive our backhandedness.
Our upchucking was an unimaginative moment, and the slowing
      down of our blood was admittedly maudlin.
Friends that we are, we know you'll forgive us our friendship.
Victor, we're marching towards you with a mind even you can't control.
Even without light, we can still make out the white, which gives us
      renewed hope and vigour.
Someone sniggers.
But we can see the road ahead, clear as our hands.
Of course, it's not a road, so much as more snow.
And, of course, our hands are no longer our hands.
And the white... the perpetual twilight is just blue enough to watch
      the wind fighting the wind.
Have we mentioned our dogs, they're feeling good enough to eat.
Not for us to eat, Victor! Don't fool around!
No need to throw us a bone Victor, we carry a sack of 'em on our backs.
No! We're not a sack of bones, Victor! Don't fool around!
It's coming true: our friendly feelings for you are extensions of our
      friendly feelings for ourselves.
Everything is possible to overcome.
Except: self-deception: self-loathing, self-love.

Cosmopolitan Double Issue

The desperate fudge, the artistic smudge.
       Those adjectives are nouns,
       those nouns are verbs.
I hope you understand:
that pause stands in for 'on the other hand'—
it isn't the caesura of apposition,
an in-breath in the aesthete's trailing list.

My point is, wisdom thrives in a softening mist,
directness being a terminal condition.
Our weirdest accidents are broadly planned—
I hope you understand.
       There's rioting in the suburbs,
       there's boredom in the towns,
the hopeful drudge, the groundless grudge.

Dark Matter

Haiku

A hundred lovers at a funeral:
trembling raindrops on a spider's web.
The ancient Japanese art of maximum-impact suicide.

Voodoo Lounge

In a jar behind the bar, a president's head.
The jungle telegraph's *kaput* :
we didn't even know he was dead.

Dawn Chorus

How consoling in the dark hours of sorrow,
this lyrical affirmation of the dawn.
And should their notes fall flat, for sure tomorrow
they'll be undeterred, the first daylit yawn

of the sleepless soul again invited
to gulp down breakfast juice of joyful song,
nourishing day by day the benighted
one with a natural remedy. Wrong!

A ruthless need primes many a dreamy wish.
Our genes rush to the mate veiled by the bride.
Beauty, always competitive, refuses to be blamed.

These birds use the dawn chorus to establish
each morning whether any of them has died
in the night, leaving a territory unclaimed.

Pilot

for *The Divine Situation Comedy*

Shared birthdays come to light in the cockpit.
Baby on board, a bonny one—keep your distance.
Ironic present of an Airfix™ kit—
glueless, disparaging. Vote of no confidence.

The baby's birthday isn't one these.
Let's christen him anyway, in pink champagne
or, better still, blue. No cloud without a breeze.
Without a prayer no wing, no luck, no plane.

GAVIN SELERIE

from *Harriot Double*

Brayne-track

Worth the journey from Duresme house,
three hours upstream by a curling line
or 9 miles as the crowe (says
my instrument on the leades
12 foote long).

Syon reach—steerage
asks *the soul*, stone within green,
what is that? Great quadrangular case
heaved from daughters' ruin.

A lone hernshaw, neck and legs stretched
flaps a powder wing in the shallows.
Horned cattle, a milk constellation
on Tide Meadow, mooze
before angle-turrets and gallery glass.

Waterstair. Ghost of Lady Jane.
Oars that dashed the creek
at rest. Winding path
to a neat walk with mulberries.

Think a whole 'arbal, knotly
layd to perfume the Aire
in freaktd order

    silverie wormewode
    branke-ursin
    whyte nesewurt
    dyshmustard
    panicke
    bellragges
    hore calamynt

wood spurge
chokefitche
horse tyme
cystbush
purple goosegrass

sovereine and strang these Doctor Turner
found by the Temmes side
or planted, for physick
(a good tryal whereof in Latin
princess Elizabeth ventured
in now the Cherye garden or orchard
half an age back)

and he the healer under Somerset's cloak,
every day more vexed with the stone,
a man hot headed to know.

Smelts they swimme up to Thistelworth—
stronde of this syde. Note in a walking scale
away from swete-lipped townsfolk
for a booke of fishes, another projected
of stones & metalles.

Anno '97 (repeat): the rose quartered in a face
begins to fade, by hard thought
phantasina you tread a sheet of white light.
Sand, gravel, steps, hall. The plot
grandly done before Adam
with eye-shafts to the court (or cloister).
From such an earl entires
bailed about to broach his device.
Grace of a name subject to few words
than much babbling.
A wave, a cryptic tag, a pewter goblet.

To Mr Heryott pension 80ˡⁱ
as graft to stock
all subjects appliable.

Lodging & laboratory,
a small house apart, at the tip
of the wall from her la: shipp's towre.
Landskip forged to convert
to gentleman. Owly-eyed, black-suited
magister of Braynford, magus
harnished wth

> greate leather-cov^d globes,
> chests of bookes of all sorts,
> furnaces in the lybrarie clossetts,
> longe table piled with papers.

Under the white crescent or half-moon
north pointed
neither servant nor officer

a skull can open
the hands unclasp to liquid gauge
the trail of stuff, its cast & rate
by pulses and paternosters.

Will you familiar rise
from the chimney-place,
chase some reason for a little event
with upright parabola, numbers split by a bar.

The heron climbs, slow and heavy,
swings along and swoops. A frog, a snake?
no, a silver fish.

Note: Braynford is an early spelling of Brentford. Thomas Harriot moved to Syon House, Isleworth, under the patronage of the ninth (Wizard) earl of Northumberland, around 1597. Earlier experiments had been conducted at Ralegh's London residence, Durham House. Syon was built on the ruins of a former abbey, part of which is currently being excavated. Lady Jane Grey went from Syon by river to be proclaimed Queen in 1553. The gardens there still bore the stamp of William Turner, herbalist and physician to Protector Somerset, called 'the father of English physique' in Harrison's Description of England (1577). Turner met the future Queen Elizabeth at Syon, c. 1549/50. Turner's son Peter probably treated Harriot's cancer in its early stages and provided advice for chemical experiments. The house where Harriot lived and worked until his death was situated to the north of the main house. The crescent or half-moon was a heraldic device of the Percys, used for instance in their book plate.

In Nomine

Ark Rawlye   Deptford, June 1587
            from Mr Chapman his yard—
by art with workemanlye care
sholde carry suche grace and countenaunce
as to terrorize the enemie.

Arke-royall   To her Majestie, January 1588
            in liewe of 5,000*li*, deabt—
for that morrice-daunce upon our waves
(this ile opprest) I thinke her
the odd shipp in the worlde for all conditiones:
no other shall make me goe out.

Anne Royal   Woolwich Dock, 29 September, 1608
            in the charge of Phineas Pett
her name re-caste by Sir Oliver Cromwell
dispight of the Kings neglect.

An hundreth foote by the keele
and thirtye seven foote broad
now sum deale overpestred & cloggd:

demy Cannon	4
Cannon perrier	4
Culverin	12
demy Culverin	16
Saker	6
port Peece	4
Fowler	4

Adamant to clappe a reckninge
that fludds agayne, smoak Morblew
through manghangled trobles.

One ghost a way from the firme slydes
sulphure suted at the close
with a shrugge of octoretye:

Bilged on her ancor, the Medway, 1636.

*Note: Ralegh, with Harriot, acquired considerable knowledge of shipbuilding technique.
Ark Rawlye, constructed for him but sold under pressure to Queen Elizabeth, became the
flagship of the English fleet which opposed the Armada.*

Arcticon

To make Terra nova: a little turret
over the Thames, with entrance on to the leades

Over my Chamber at Durham house,
the measured levell square
(accounting half the thickness of the wall
which casteth in the rayne)
within which the rayne falleth
to runne out of the spoute in the corner
is 268¾ foote square, after this manner

My cube of brasse whose internall side 3 inches
conteyneth of rayne water
iust full by eye as it is even by the sides
& playned by a ruler ounces of
troye   14 ± ½ ± $\frac{1}{16}$
Being filled more till it began to runne
over the side being wet for it,
it conteyned now   14 ± ½ ± $\frac{1}{16}$
That experiment had error for I found after
it had leaked & therefore I proved agayne
the leakes being stopped, it is full
with iust   troy   14 ± ½

A beat of the pulse one second gives
8½ inches p. 24 hr

Calls the brain to fathom how
to take traverse on fish-track, the stickle current
all a vaster league
in growley squall & thicke fogge

your rutter hath not the cutts
your almanack may not tally
nor compasse fall right

How to know your course to sayle
to any place assigned
& in sayling to keep to make true reckoning
to find where you are
& how farre from any place desired

Surplus of the Horizon (table in minutes)
to correct for the Hight of the ey
above the water in pases (one pase being 5 foot).
Elevation of the pole from meridian altitude of the Sonne.
A figure shewing when the guardes are in rule.
Allowances of the pole starre.
Regiment of the Sonne.
Amplitudes of the Sonne.

The astrolabe, his agitation & unquiet hanging.
The sea ringe's scale twice as large
but tossed again. Excentricity of the [cross] staffe.

By sea marriadge these will agree
as sonne & starre
and more nearly p.fect a maryners plott

Note: At Ralegh's instigation, Harriot prepared sailors for voyages to the New World.
Arcticon is the title of his lost manual on ships and navigation. A range of notes and
related papers survive.

You Are the Designer

Are you loitering with
intent? These forms need
to be overflowing with
information. Here is an
eco-system unlike any
other, more than a million
square miles of shallow
but never stagnant water.
For the first time in history,
large numbers of people
regularly travel out of
their habitual surroundings.
You could save the other
half until later yet this
creature tends to dominate
its environment, killing
and maiming unselectively.
Are you loitering with intent?
Part of our timidity arises
from our unwillingness
to offend anybody but this
may be about to change.
Next time around he simply
flooded the terrain with data.
Subject to certain controls,
recreational activities on
this reservation may continue.
Are you loitering with intent?

An Unconventional Wisdom

It's disconcerting that a man
so confident with his voice
should be so diffident and
meek physically. Then again,
this claim may be wishful
thinking or plain wrong.
He was wearing black eye-
liner and Doc Marten boots,
yet this is hardly a trivial
matter, despite the fact that
she danced all night and
shopped all day. Who are
the top predators in our
micro-world? "When I,
Aguirre, want the birds to
drop dead from the trees,
then the birds will drop dead
from the trees." Don't
be deterred by the weather—
service is speedy and the
batter makes it worth waiting
all day. Gucci, meanwhile,
drove the message home
with a slick collection of
flattering low-rise trousers.
His objections, in general,
proved to be of the most
trifling and technical kind.

A Smoother Appearance

In preparing a deal the
city took a long, hard
look at the books yet
life here is dictated
by the tides, the seasons
and the weather. In
the formal image the
couple are standing
close together and both
are smiling at the camera.
This is a really deadly
presentation which also
works in clear water.
Over-fishing might
contribute to a sudden
increase in shark
attacks yet intimate
behaviours, like dense-
roosting, allows the
fungus to spread. We
may yet see something
similar in the far reaches
of our solar system. Where
there is violence, sex is
never far away.

4 *Poems from* Tea and Small Bones

If you are bitten at noon
no aspect of a feather
will stop the womb its flooding
like how darkness will leave
its gracefully carved labia
when washed from its slope.

Between sunset and rise
the quiet grows redder
a drowsy, arythmic dance that
slips a skin right past its body
so near she can almost feel it
like a memory's spine.

No prior experience with migration
can prepare you for this night
its architecture of gaps
a moth-eaten moon
fallen into its sun
and no way to know
if a sleeper will take your dream.

*

Evacuated and bored
the bone strings itself
amongst the beads and settles against
your neck, prepared to winter.

You'll dig the pit but it will win,
the earth not bothered by the blemish.
Your fire burns the lovely just as well—
seal the womb from fresh air and poise.

Viscid and potioned with curtains drawn,
just scraped scabs on her tongue
the healer hang fired and ready
for her incisions to submit to his fork.

Your injections can't pierce this cocoon—
bite me to a bruise and spit my skin.

*

Meet the fire dawn at her breaking.
Risked with holy yellow light.

Swallow what she'll offer.
Taste the bitter of her month.

Weave prayer through her tangles.
Promise against her tongue.

Push velvet through the rind.
A fleshly melon for your burst.

She'll ride fertile to tomorrow.
And will leave him on the verge.

Sand sticking to your moist.
Your fruit in a jar.

*

Sacrifice a hammer to the evening
and wrap your braids around her torso.
Dig a hole and drain your ribbons in the earth.
Exits ought to be pretty and complete.
They are eaten by grown-ups
and children alike.

The bitemarks on your lip will expose you
when he sneaks up like that—
backlit, innocent and eerie.
Circle his question with your damp
skin and make an example of it.
Embed a pearl in your button
and gloss your own quiver.

It is a very high window.
You will love him to the smash.
He'll leave no damage, a sideways signature,
and a thought he can't fold.
In front of his hands floats a gesture,
her eyes cotton and honest.

Listening to Fallujah

1. White Phosphorous and High Explosives

In Fallujah a rain of fire fell on the city,
very sparingly, for Illumination Purposes.

We fired 'shake and bake' at the insurgents
using Willy Pete to flush them out

and H.E. to take them out
of trench lines and spider holes.

It burns ... It's an incendiary weapon ...
That is what it does.

I saw the burned bodies of women and children.
It melts the flesh all the way down to the bone.

Indirect Fires in the Battle of Fallujah by Captain James T. Cobb, First
Lieutenant Christopher A. La Cour and Sergeant First Class William H. Hight.
March–April 2005 *Field Artillery*

Fallujah: the Hidden Massacre, Italian State Documentary RAI, Mohamad
Tareq, biologist in Fallujah, and former American soldier Jeff Englehart

Willy Pete – white phosphorous H. E. - High Explosives

2. Little is known

In Fallujah little is known
about the types of weapons deployed,

about post-war contamination
of mutagenic carcinogens,

oil fires, heavy metals and
uranium from weapons,

but reports began to emerge after 2005
of a sudden increase in cancers and leukaemia's

a remarkable reduction of males
born one year after

and an increase in birth defects,
infant death and malignancies

the results reported here
do not throw any light upon the identity of the agent(s)

and although we have drawn attention
to the use of depleted uranium

as one potential relevant exposure,
there may be other possibilities.

Cancer, Infant Mortality and Birth Sex-Ratio in Fallujah, Iraq 2005–2009
Chris Busby, Malak Hamdan and Entesar Ariabi. *International Journal of
Environmental Research and Public Health* ISSN 1660-4601 www.mdpi.com/
journal/ijerph

3. Question 618

There is a constant dynamic lessons learned process
about all sorts of things militarily.

There are operational level lessons relating to Fallujah
to do with command and control,
to do with precision targeting,
precision use of weaponry in built-up areas,
and all those sorts of things.

The strategic lessons about Fallujah
have got to be bespoke
to a particular issue or incident
within an overall campaign.

The assessments for determining
whether or not it was a correct political thing
to prosecute the clearance of Fallujah or not
were essentially political in nature, not military.

Clearly Fallujah had taken on
some totemic type stature
as a safe environment for insurgents.

One could say in retrospect
the political decision vis-à-vis Fallujah
was the correct one.

Wednesday 9 February 2005
Examination of Witnesses Select Committee on Defence
Minutes of Evidence
MAJOR GENERAL NICK HOUGHTON CBE

Red Hibiscus

Once as Bone Monkey walked the forest paths
a travelling man appeared and spoke to him.

Which of these packets will you have? He asked,
raising two parcels for our friend to choose.

The first was large, imposing, wrapped in leaves
and dressed with a red hibiscus bloom.

*This one has knives, a looking glass and beads
paper and ink, cloth, all you could need.*

The other package swung from his little finger
wrapped in rough cloth and smaller than his thumb.

Immortal Life he said, *is held within
and you can take which bundle you would like.*

I'll have the largest, please Bone Monkey said
and straightaway unwrapped the gift,

picked out the prettiest knife, to test the blade,
and plunged it in his benefactor's chest.

I'll take the smallest too, he told his host
and stole it from the dead man's open palm.

The Blacksmith made me

With blazing tongs he clamped my head
and cut it off, sliced up my flesh and jointed me.
As big as half the earth, a cauldron hung above his fire.
He threw me in the pot to make his stew.

So three years passed – I simmered and my fat
rose to the surface and was skimmed away.

Next day he ladled out my bones and working fast
he put them in his fire below the coals
and when I blanched and spat he took me
to his anvil and he struck three massive blows.

And then I sang. I was a bell
and when he plunged me in his trough I was the sea.

The blacksmith made me who I am. He took
my naked bones and covered them. My skull was bare,
his iron hand put in obsidian eyes and lanced my ears,
so down through all the years I'd imitate the speech of man.

GERARD GREENWAY

Worldless = winter = bareness

Worldless =
winter =
bareness

Stand out there
midst the
warm outside
on the ground, grass
around you hive
of foliage
warm nimbus
of swarm of
small leaves
with glaucous underside
shadow depths
inside

Don't stay
here
back against
an earthing
plate
that makes you
the bare
unvibranced
—unwarmthed
unfoliaged
unsurrounded
in warm
surrounding air
—unsuffused with
liquid current
that takes you
up on
out

Stand out there
midst the
warm outside

World =
summer, spring =
burgeoning

Father

I reach out to
his facing elsewhere
to his knowing but
unknowing, to his
seeing but unseeing
in his negative
absorption, his
eyes tight closed
his face moon-dust
grey, moon-light
lit, his hair
soft and astray
blankly gently
nestled in himself
half flesh half
space, in his
length his girth
rotating gently
spinning away

The word, the days

The word
that speaks of
the days
how different
it is
to the longness
of the days
to their
stillness, paleness
and
expanse

The word that
speaks the truth
of the days
how nonned
its truth
by the days

The word
that makes
resolve
how distant
is its closeness
in the distance
of the
days

Spiritual Letters (Series 6, #4)

After school, he was entering the train station to travel home to South Melbourne when he was stopped by a drunken Scandinavian sailor, who asked him to light his cigarette for him and then stroked his hair with shaking hands. The boy tried to get into a different carriage, walking quickly down the platform when the train arrived, but the sailor followed after and chided him. *During one visit she showed me an antique stereopticon she'd bought at a flea market, complete with several boxes of the glass slides, all very old photos of various oddities and exotica from all over the world. It was dirty and rusty and basically inoperable but I was totally fascinated with it . . .* We ate breakfast together: bratwurst, boiled eggs and pumpernickel with butter.—I didn't think your friend's wife would look like that, his girlfriend said when he showed her the photographs from his holiday abroad.—Look more closely, he replied; that's not his wife, it's me. He had a remote viewer engaged to try to track his journey, with the viewer in a completely white room somewhere in London and he in an undisclosed, faraway country. While not, he said, having any belief in it, or against it, but intrigued by the idea. As we walked down the street, a van stopped and six policemen climbed out; they forced us against a wall and searched us, allegedly for drugs. When one of them asked my friend what he had under his cap, he said: My brains.—My brother's a professor, and he'd spit on you, the woman at the next table said, apparently outraged by our bookish talk.—You're so rude, she continued, someone should kill you; I think *I'll* kill you. He told me about the exploits of the Ninja, and later bought me a Ninja suit to wear when I appeared with him. *They travelled in disguise to other territories to judge the situation of the enemy, they would . . . enter enemy castles and set them on fire, and carried out assassinations, arriving in secret.*—What have you been doing recently? I asked.—I've been practising shape shifting. We were taken aback to find that he, with his love of marble, limestone, gilded terra-cotta and brass, glass spheres and gold, had been buried in a cemetery in Old Cairo with a tin can as a marker, flattened and written on with a felt-tip pen. *Men who humble themselves to worship things preserved by human skill commit sin: such are but the cold carving of stone, dry wood, hard metal, or dead bones. Deprive them of your veneration, and, since they are unfeeling, they will be defiled by dogs and crows.* Fragile pyramid, newspaper and wire mesh; branches in leaf pushing through the walls. I wondered about the possibility of a soft pyramid. *For the protection of the head of the mummy . . . layers of linen and papyrus glued together and stiffened with gesso, moulded and painted in the likeness of the human face, were introduced* . . . I was shown a photograph of a woman they claimed was my wife, with cuts on her face.—It's good to see that we're taking such a shit off the streets. On his last night in the small village by the sea he went to a pub and sat reading Keats, across the room from a group of skinheads.—Did they walk on water, as it was said?—No, nor did they become invisible. When the two policewomen arrested me, they called me by someone else's name, and took me in front of a senior officer who showed me a photograph of hands that were supposedly mine.—See, they don't look like mine at all, I said, but the two women replied that they really did. Until the end of his life he will keep a painting of *a reclining woman whose face has been ferociously obliterated.* You can see the little boy's reflection on the side of the car, as he reaches to touch the door handle. A young woman in a straw hat and a young man are in the front seats; an older man—the woman's and the boy's father—sits in the back. Blood dashed from a bucket over the decaying carcass of beef, for its colour's sake—for the painting's sake. Large blue flies gathering around, chased away, gathering again. Walking along the shore at night, I passed the sea cadet club where a dance was in full swing, everyone dressed in their uniforms and some older girls dancing with young male cadets.—I don't know how you could be an artist, she said, and never visited Norfolk. He has publicly championed the younger man's paintings, writing a monograph on his art . . . praising him in rapturous, almost delirious, yet apt prose. His daughter will decline an offer of marriage from the artist; while her father will no longer be on speaking terms with him. In the dream a strange animal spat out pieces of manuscript in my face, then, shaking itself, shed or lost its spines. A workman in paint smeared overalls grabbed me by the arm and pulled me back from an oncoming car.—I'll see you tomorrow! he called out as we went separate ways—as if he somehow expected me to be there at the same time every day.—Someone commented that his friend, the mathematician and cartographer, had a mind like a spice merchant's.—A compliment, of course. ...*your gaze prompts me to consider how this image of your face is thus portrayed in a sensible fashion since a face could not have been painted without colour and colour does not exist without quantity. Your true face is absolute from every contraction.* He stood gazing at the small boats—white and blue or white and black—in the still, smooth water; the rocks near the shore were clearly visible, but the boats were less distinct the further away in the fog, and the island in the distance a mere spectral smudge.

JOHAN DE WIT

Becky

When going out, Becky always looked around, because, as she said, the environment is never the same, it can change from one day to the next and if it can it will and as I only go out once a day it is an absolute certainty that it will have changed the next day that's why I look around because I'd like to know where I am; if I don't know where I am I may attribute change to the wrong place and if I do that then I can't find my way back home. As you can see, Becky's logic is impeccable, but Becky also created a narrative and that caused a problem down the line where Becky was born anti-narratively and because she was born like that she'd grown up like that. Her parents had done their best, her teachers had done their most, her friends had done their upmost and her lovers had done their upbeat best but Becky remained anti-narrative with an impeccable logic on her lips. So, wherever Becky went, she wanted to erase narrative, that's why she bought razor blades by the dozen, although these come in packs of five or ten which is really a nuisance when you need them by the dozen because going from one to the other you need to be skilled in factorisation and before you know it you do sums all day long and are back at narrative through the back door and she wanted to avoid all that and that could only be done by erasing each narrative at a time by using a fresh razor blade each time. That's why Becky went out only once a day, because razor blades cut both ways, which way up is a matter of trial and error; by then it might be too late to go out again.

Samantha

Samantha, as we already know, had tried more than once to get rid of her obsession to get rid of an obsession had become an obsession. But let's have lunch first: bread, cottage cheese, herring, an apple and redbush tea. Samantha, as we also already know, changed her mind after every meal about what to do about her obsession; three meals a day but only one obsession, the one she wanted to get rid of, that is. So if Samantha is to get rid of her obsession it has to happen before the next meal. Samantha, you better hurry. A quick résumé: Samantha, obsession, next. When I go to the door I check whether the door is open or locked before I open the door and when I close the door I have to check whether the door was open or locked before I close the door. Sometimes this happens a dozen times a day, and obviously a dozen times takes time and during that time I can't do anything else and that's a real pity because there is so much to do. How much time have I got? Ah, as tomorrow is another day I'll try again. Samantha! Yes? Tomorrow might be another day, could you do it now? Right, although tomorrow is day enough now I have to do it. Samantha went to the door and decided it was closed. Samantha looked over her shoulder to see whether the narrator would confirm her observation but it was too dark. To lock her observation in her mind so she could use it for the next step she cried out loud: the door is closed! She quickly stepped into action. She unlocked the door, crossed the threshold, closed the door and screamed: the door is closed!

Charlie

Charlie went back to work. That's what he did, year in year out. And each year he waited until after August bank holiday which according to his latest diary, a WHS A63, is called Late Summer Holiday. Awful, absolutely awful for a day to be given such a name, and because Charlie couldn't stand the sound of that name he always ended up banking on August bank holiday. Two thirds of the year is gone, it's time to go back to work! On his way to work two things occurred to him: one, I'm on my way to work and two, I'm going back to work; and then a third thought flashed by: things and thoughts are one when work turns your back to work. Charlie was making good progress: his legs were moving; his mood was square and his mind was held in check by purpose, pitfalls and proteins. Almost halfway! I must have made the right decision. Decisions being his weakest point Charlie got nervous. Let's do some imaging! Charlie looked over his shoulder, his left one as his right one was too stiff. Is somebody following in my footsteps, why does the sound my new trainers leave behind keep ringing my ears? They ought to know that gadgets are not a part of my imaginary toolbox. Charlie looked at his feet, counting one two, one two. Almost there! With his eyes open, his arms in full swing and his legs finding the right direction Charlie approached his office, looked at his watch: ten to nine, I'm early, looked at the door and read: hazard zone—do not cross! Ah, better luck next year, Charlie whispered, then turning round he turned round and round.

from Culbone Wood Journal

It is morning and on the table lie the two sheets on which the last afternoon's composition is indited. How deep that vision was. How distant, broad in scope and unwontedly complete. But how arcane its topography. The golden sun-glozed dome still glows—as though gold leaf beaten to an ultimately airy thinness mantles the intelligence—and there, cooled by a breeze from the northwestern steppe, ample spaces gather to the palace and stretch thence through Asia. Below the dome the Great Khan with his concubines perambulate. Conducted by an *Abyssinian*, who sings to lull it, a dark spotted pard on a gold chain walks behind them.

(What, this attempt to alchemise such, latter, allusive phraseology? Forced gold! Fool's gold! And for this reason. However-so-far the Khan's power stretched from Cathay to the Baltic, *Africa* lay beyond even his great empire's reach. That *Abyssinian* derives from ignorance of history, which falseness renders it anachronistic. Notwithstanding this, the term has arrived for its convergence of both like and unlike vowels and consonants. And these, in turn, suggest that word of Biblical immensity, *abyss*—with its near suggestion of *abysm* from *The Tempest*—whose proximity is haunting.)

*

Now as I write, I have not yet revisited the pages which are the product of my *prophetic fury* (I have shifted to Othello's Sibyl, O judicious critick!) For the circumstances of the phantasmagoria still live in my waking. And on this quotidian October morning, I am there now in *Xanadu* and would, were I able, immortalise the enchantment. Yet when I stretch my hand to position my ink horn, the quill dies in my fingers. My forearm is forestalled. I raise my left hand, bring it onto my brow, touch the fingers to a temple. This is daily Somersetshire bristle—unharvested. For am I not simply that hapless self that laboured yesterday through mud and briars—and in the flux of his own excrement—to collapse in retreat among these hospitable premises? And am not I also that Tom O'Bedlam who entreated

From the hag and hungry goblin
            That into rags would rend ye . . .
    In the book of moons defend ye . . . ?

How close this touches! Xanadu and Bedlam lie adjacent in me.

*

I have breakfasted on a ham, and now in bustles the farmhouse maid to carry off my dishes and to mend the grate. Up reaches a flame. And now a second. The tongues parry and embrace, fall, jostle on each other, withdraw into the timber, crawl against the bark as though clutching for a hold. The girl kneels at the hearth and builds in logs of ash wood and apple. Who reinvented this blaze? Who re-ignites it?

"Pardon, Sir?" as though she overhears my enquiry.
"Go, child," I reply. "It is nothing." The girl thanks me. I know not for what. But as she passes through the door, I call her.
"Pray," I ask, without knowing what I intend and without premeditation, "Can you sing, lady?"
"Why yes, sir. All about here have songs of the neighbourhood. And the hymns we do in chapel." (A curious locution, "do", and not unhappy.)
"Then as you go about your household duties—not here, mind, by me—will you, time to time, give voice to any song you might, in the ordinary way, sing at your own hearth or with neighbours?"

Suspecting me to be mad, as well I might be, the girl withdrew. A whispered consultation followed (I surmise with her mistress). And there ensued a silence all that morning so much deeper than any I have experienced, so that (besides this renewal of *flamboyance* in the grate) all I could hear was the singing in my ears and the sound of the still air on me in the parlour as, in my indolence, I moved between chairs and tarried—with some expectation of a compositional renewal—by the table.

And all this time, at a tree by a river, with a thin bridge to traverse it, a black, solitary damsel stands. She cries through the

89

dusk and a slow wind stirs the instrument she carries. At each short flurry, a dulcet and exotic tone arises: as if in the night air, sound became a prism and was lifted through the twilit glimmer.

*

How gorgeous was that vision. And how insubstantial its outcome. Here in muddy Somerset I squat with this trickle of the gilded river I envisaged dried up in the dirty morning twilight, while in some remote fastness of an Asian landscape that thick gold goes for ever rushing. I *go* to the table. But those pages cease to draw me. They are thin, poor objects. Paper merely. The good solid things in this parlour have more substance, usefulness and durability than those pale leaves afloat on the sustaining table surface. Old workings of oak, hewn in Devon last century. A dark, pewter tankard, coppers, and the tongs and shovels that lie inert at the hearth with its coals still aglow in a mountain range of ashes. See too the ravines inside this, pocked with caverns, faery dells and casements, shaggy humps and tumuli which let fall now and then their own substance.

The beamed ceiling of this room is low and, of a sudden, the oppressive architecture of this rural heaven, as though to threaten my thought and obliterate my vision, all too low. And my quill, as I write this, falters. It is heavy in my fingers. This is a feather that may never ascend again.

*

It is chance, but not entirely, that led me to the Great Khan's palace. Chance that I entered my reverie at a moment when I faced that one page: and yet I have confidence that it was destiny that guided me. I was there in Cathay on account of previous excursions through the pages of Purchas. But this was not my first acquaintance with the Great Khan and his lands and people. These I knew already through Marco. The writings of old travellers have long drawn me to accompany them on their peregrinations (this word in compliment to Purchas: for I take it as a sign that all the voyages of which he give account are called pilgrimages, in that they seek, as it were, a shrine, some holy palace of truth: albeit through what he interprets as a pagan wasteland—which for ever will be the outworks of a Christendom to which he believes all mankind are destined.)

Cathay was therefore already in the landscape of my dreaming. But all *oneiric* travel is haphazard. Chimeras, sea beasts, messengers from the sky, chthonic apparitions, heavenly cities and a vast topography of infernal landscapes populate the ancient mind as is evidenced in Homer, Hesiod, Virgil, Ovid, *Genesis* and *Revelation*. All these converge in our own imaginings. And fitted round the fables thrown forth by the dreamers, seers and poets who have sung these fancies, is an ancient world which is still half our own—there is an Italy and Greece, an Euphrates delta, China—and half coloured by the shades and pigments, geographic histories, lights and shadows drawn by the ancients. Like sun on a ruin, a bank of cloud above a hill, or the scent of thyme carried by a summer wind over the heath: so these actualities are given transient redolence and bloom and, in combination, suffuse the volume of a totality on which the imagination feeds. Or to adopt another figure: there is, on the one hand, the verifiable architecture with its geological grain and the musical formality of its interrelated parts which communicates a harmonious effusion into the landscape in which it is placed. Marble thus received by hills and trees throws out towards these what I may call, in its old sense, *glamour*, which nature in turn reciprocates. So the mind apprehends the objects of perception and by a process of exchange creates scenes of unprecedented moods and fancifully charmed features which is present actuality and the agency of imagination in congruence.

Literature and the traditions of popular narrative are thus wilderness and garden compounds. Any visit into this brings about mental changes, but also an enriched familiarity. It is both savage and cultivated, impenetrable and all embracing. We enter the maze and get used to becoming lost. And when we can not escape, there we must camp and sometimes perish. The labyrinth itself, indeed, is a summation and fulfilment of a paradox. We enter both in order to find the centre—which is a salvation—and to leave. If we leave we are bereft an enclosure, however terrifying this. It is not a freedom that we can easily endure. We long once again for the embrace of those narrow lanes of wall whose sides lean in towards us so threateningly. We miss the familiarity of secondarily breathed air. It is a purgatorial treadmill. We stumble in Dante's sandals on those twisting escarpments: the rocks' pressure sharp, the path progressively more austere, as they ascend the Empyrean.

*

All poetic endeavour has its origin and indeed its context in one thing and idea. It is rooted in the *Fall* and our continuing interaction with 'that forbidden tree', whose blossom and fruit still inform consciousness and existence. All song and poetic utterance proclaim a celebration of the orchard in whose cradle we were rocked for that sweet, short single day of our moral gestation—but from which we have since been in exile. But to sing of Paradise is also to lament our exclusion from that darling infant dream. And so all poetry must be double in its character. We can know nothing but glimpses and intuitions of that inaccessible *pardes* (the Hebrew, I think, is from Persian). And our singing proceeds from the daily experience of exile in a world which can never become more than unsatisfactory.

That mighty, but all too laconic, poem that initiates the Hebrew *Genesis* presents us with the paradigm or model of all our discomforts. And our rhythmic murmurings and cries, expostulations, ratiocinations and effusions, even our brief, ecstatic shafts of light and music (shot through as these must be with consciousness of our mortality) represent a variation of that primal sorrow: As hourly we repeat in countless measures our mythical first parents' bondage—as they stood before it—to that shining and sanctified perfect tree of both enlightenment and disillusion. One moment, they stood, albeit at a distance, separate and content to gaze with awe at that sacred other element of the comfortable home they must know only partially. The next, with the apple in their hands and soon within their bodies, they became as we are, separated from their perfection.

Having thus incorporated what, at the centre, they had been forbidden, they must carry this same thing into exile with them. A fate we have inherited and whose reverberation we perpetuate. Indeed, all action is to re-*verb*, re-enact and express anew in constant variation that fatal, first, self-alienation.

*

In answer to the above: All this of course is metaphor, and by 'the Fall' I mean the phenomenon of *variability*. For the prelapsarian was static, and our first parents made the reasonable and dynamic choice. This was neither a sin nor a mistake and has been called, I think, a *felix culpa*. At the moment that they reached for the apple, this was the point at which they became human, for the *noli tangere* command was stultifying, and through an eternity of obedience they would have lived in servitude. By transgressing, on the other hand, they asserted their true nature. And in wagering loss against an unknowable, albeit painful freedom, they chose mortality over the pieties of a sterile and undying sabbath. In doing thus, they revolted against perfection—for this courage I applaud them. And if, as a result, the fruit must be germinated only to decompose, then we must glory and participate in that susceptibility. This globe we inhabit is a fruit that feeds, after all, on the compost of its alternating cycles. And I am content to contribute my own rot to the general. (It was, I am told by a traveller from some far eastern desert, a fig tree, not an apple, in the Persian paradise. Did our parents defecate incontinently, and for this pollution were excluded from the garden?!)

*

I may not claim to have chosen, volitionally, the subject, place or form of my poem. Truer to say that its subject and context chose to enter me, and that resulting from this traffic, the composition process—as yet teasingly obscure to my understanding—would appear to have taken place over three distinct stages.

The first came with my perusal of that paragraph in Purchas (albeit I might at the time have been reading any other part of the volume which I have scanned daily). The second stage lay in the penetration of this matter to some remote situation of occluded or unconscious thought. And it was in such a place, crystallising in a region of the hidden imaginative faculty, that the organism of the poem, autonomously, autochthonously, and even perhaps cthonically, of itself developed, evolving, as it were, within a ductile or malleable geologic stratum and must continue in that condition until such time as it was excavated in the next waking moment. The third stage lay with the return of consciousness, during which my hand, as though at dictation from a voice coming from memory (mine, albeit strange to me, mining the ore of a still indistinct *Meinung*!), inscribed the lines that lie before me on this all too actual morning on a farmhouse table.

Here we have, perhaps, a model of the imaginative activity. The stimulating factor having its inception in some concrete eventuality, which latter is then transferred in dream through the body and the mind, as though these latter constituted a processing medium in which volition had no role. The time, the place, the accidents of detail being transformed as the stimulating matter passes like a subterranean stream of that same precious and occluded ore until it issues onto paper where finally it stays—exiguous and coldly, as transcribed in daylight! The person or character of the creative agent (that self which has a name, a history and future), the operation of the will and intellection, were therefore passive. Involuntary reflex, alone, lent shape to the issue. Although these materials emerged in the shape of *language* is a sign or a mark of the impress of the human on this compositional process. The body and the mind in this respect may be compared to the experimental locus of a reaction. As I sow vegetable seed or plant a fruit tree, those will develop so long as their environment remains benign. Given soil, light and water, the organism can not but thrive. Nor does my lamp burn from its desire to radiate. Poetry, in a comparable manner, emerges through the impress of some internal bodily and intellectual mould through which the inspiriting material has been introduced, whether or not this will be the matter of what eventuates finally in consciousness.

13 Poems

My body is a grove of olives. Touch me
where I'm hurt, on the ferny pubis. Insects without eyes
have emptied me of fruits. What I grow is nothing.
Not even madness. Take me, a wound-labyrinth.
One gets used to being born in many different tombs.
Closer to my lips climbs
the erection of silence

*

All the dead have a right to the dark. Come through
this flesh—this coffin with two shadows. I shall be the forgetting
of the voyage that is you. I shall be your creation.
To measure the human species what's needed is a tree.

*

I've served their desert up on my plate. That's all they've
got on offer. And that's all you lose. Sand, grit, stones.
Hardly any water. I'm nailed to my thirst. I devour
your absence. The crossings aren't where we thought.

*

The sperm of history fecundates no tree.
There are women like cities. Burnt.
Their ovaries charred in each act of abandon.

*

Under the skin, our laughter is a cactus.
There's kerosene in our blood and soon enough—
very soon, the UN will be inspecting our orifices.
For it's in them we're accused of harbouring
chemical substances.

*

Thanks to men the sky writes nothing. Half
of fire is made of ink. Your brain in my loins
chases my ashes. And all those words—all those words
hung on the posts where we are whipped.

*

Our eyelids force death upon us.
It isn't our souls, this Babel within us. A lock, perhaps?
Your dust pours chaos onto my gums. Your opposite
plants your lips on my crumbling. For a tunnel in your arms
I've bartered my hips to one glad to be blind. And the wall for a window.
Your cries gave birth to my mouth. The sky
in our throats is liquid. Open.

*

They put my head in a hole. And the hole
in a bottle. And took the bottle to court.
And accused the hole of being a hole. And me
of filling it. How can you fill a hole
with a nothing?

*

Don't tell me you love me. The verb is a death.
And the word—a wall with no lizards.

*

When your hips fall you plough across me.
A landscape unattained. You borrow me from my thirst.
It takes our thighs to make a silence. You spell me. Unbeknown
to me, you pronounce me. It's in our rooms that we pretend.
Prolong me with an absent gesture.

*

Applaud at fixed times. Drink your soup through your nostrils.
Weep to order on alternate days. Masturbate your daffodils
only if it brings in cash. Your blood must take you back
to your gash. Undomiciled in your brain, your heart is a fern
within the guts of fire. Your every step gives birth to a hole. To a sky
reduced to whiplash its own migration. The sea is nothing more
than its own horizon. It's all to do with verticals.
Ladders. Windows. Humans.

*

This bed is too narrow for our nakednesses. It's the pavement
you hug, with the din of other people. And all this Braille within us
is poured into concrete. It's not our shadows but the wall that's
        moving on.
At noon you lose me and find me again in stone. You bring me back
a movement from the memory of walls. I didn't recognise my gate
        or my grave.
The universe—just another word in the blood. You're throttling me.
        My throat—
the sepulchre of your fire. Mar me with your rod. I accept my face now.

*

Plenty—a blow job for the sand. My flesh is the sister of want.
Tell me why our chairs have thirteen crutches and a single leg if I die
in any case—of apnoea in the void. Through the crack you came in
an abyss thrusts me out. They're rolling joints with our asphyxiations.
It's forever noon on our flanks, same place same time.
There aren't any lovers. There are the drowned, turned into rivers.
Then there is your tear. My love your tear is my burden.

CHRISTINE MARENDON   *TRANSLATED BY KEN COCKBURN*

Boonies

In the morning, the whole team
gathered round my bed. Questions:
Is it ten when the bird comes?
Do the pyramids smile? Blue, such
blue plums. And the iguana?

Rattling milk-teeth, peewits, the lot. And
what does a house consist of? Have you
been to the desert? In a northerly direction, till
the needle trembles and breaks. Straight ahead,
straight ahead, there's my house, there's my bed.

No, I'm not telling.

A green arrow and even his shirt
lacks buttons. A king, enthroned there, says:
red and blue are mine. Bends his knee.
The cord's all knotted. Maybe, ten,
yes, ten. He'll be back tomorrow.

Terrestre

This is the same path, the same trail
and the river . . . it might be said
it moves as it always does, indeed the
flock of birds appears as if on cue
above this stand of trees, which reliably
lose leaves and recur. It's always me
in the field here checking co-ordinates;
the time inbetween never passes other than as always
now; the air, shredded. I stick, as well as I can,
to this vantage point, which seems to me no different
under the earth than from this place;
stone under water. Something might lead out above it,

to the town, to a country, road-signs switched round, or
onto the stone, this leaf, a sea? It's been a while
since I believed this memory was even mine.

Bewitching

Walking night after night through
walls which breathe in and out more deeply
than someone dying. Fevered foreheads
press against window-panes. So much
is awake and a tongue there licks
the silver spoon of medicine.

I walk, with you and you. And
the riddle: how many are we, two,
or three, or five? The house-count's so high
in town in the morning. The way
whales spout fountains the sun
rises and then the stars and

lastly the moon. Everything's there,
but see the words, don't trust them.

They lie in heaps and remain
dreams. And when at night they
cross streams, your hear their names.

Stellaria

Useless prayers, when you sleep there's nothing
threatens you. You polish metal, basketfuls
of the weirdest bits and pieces you can't
fit together. Which mechanism,
if you had the know-how, which
machine? It could be a rifle
or an astronomical telescope. Black
smudges all over the cloth, tonight
heavenly bodies, fired upon, will fall.

CHANTAL MAILLARD

TRANSLATED BY
ANAMARÍA CROWE SERRANO

Spindle-Poems

ONE

One.
Because there are more.
More outside.
Outside the room.
Outside the other rooms.
Outside the house.
The house is too big.
They spread as I sleep.
Because there are many of them too.
Lately they're in bad repair.
Damp. Blind.
It depends on the day.
It depends on the clouds.
On the images too.
In particular, it depends on the threads.

Leaving means taking steps outside.
Outside the room.
Not the mind:
there is none. There's thread.
Leaving means taking steps
outside the room with thread.
The same thread.

Sometimes the thread
snaps. Because it's weak,
or because the other room
is dark. By
mistake, we pull and it breaks.
Then there's silence.

But there's no silence.
Not while you say so.
There's none. There's thread,
another thread.
The word silence inside.
Inside one—one?

THREADS

The flesh remains—to remain?—
wounded. There's a scar.

And the mind—the mind?—wounded.
Wounded? No, there's no wound. If
there were there'd be blood. There's
a scar. Not that either.
It would be obvious if there were
a scar. You can't always see them, it seems.
Certain words are used
instead of others, it seems. When
there aren't enough words.
Better when there's no
thing.

The mind acknowledges feelings:
segregates. It threads. Not the mind. There is none.
There's only thread. Saliva.

The dry mouth. There's no saliva. Is
there not? A thread forms an image. The
image of a body. White. Like
all the bodies who've died. I haven't
seen it. I've seen others. Not that one. But
it forms an image. The thread. Something segregates.

Hunger. Something says
hunger. Sates it. Cold?

Something remembers the word
cold. Doesn't feel it. Obviates it.

I'll have to get up. Though
without knowing what for. Without
knowing why the what for.
Get up and walk around this
room. Or also go to some o-
ther room. But no. It's safer
to stay here, typing. A keyboard
is something known. They make
an odd sound, the keys,
when you press them.
Stay in the known.
—Stay?—Remain. I already said
remain. Already asked.
To stay is to remain
for a shorter period.
You can always leave.
Leaving means taking steps outside.
Outside the room.
Not the mind.—Mind?-
I already asked. And there's none. There's thread.

Leaving is taking steps
outside the room
with thread. The same thread.
The word silence inside.
Inside one—one?

Explosion of the Marsh Marigold

Storm yellow
Like the leer of Amazons
Filled with the lust of chrome
The pregnant marsh marigold rises
From the ancestral pond
Exploding
The solitude of the gods

The laughter of the larks makes me shudder.

Bloodhound

Bloodhound at my heart
Who guards my fire
Who feeds on bitter kidneys
In the suburb of my misery

With the wet flame of your tongue
Lick the salt of my sweat
Sugar of my death

Bloodhound in my flesh
Retrieve the dreams that flee from me
Bark at the white ghosts
Bring all my gazelles
Back to their fold

And bite the ankles of my runaway angel

Written in the Hospice
December 1949 to January 1950

Did I pluck you in the gardens of Ephesus
The curly hair of your carnations
The evening bouquet of your hands?

Did I fish for you in the lakes of dream
An angler on your meadows' shores
I threw you my heart for food

Did I find you in the dryness of the desert
You were my last tree
You were the last fruit of my soul

Now I am wrapped in your sleep
Bedded deep in your repose
Like the almond in its night-brown shell

The Fear-Dancer

The fear in your hands is light as smoke over fields
You are caught in a tower of thorns
You glide through its walls yet you never find your way to me

The fear in your hair is yellow as the glow of dying candles
The fear in your voice is inscrutable as fog
You hurl yourself against my breast and yet I cannot feel you

You are a fear dancer disguised as autumn crocus
In a circle of red warriors you are buoyed by the music of bones
Yet you never break the circle and you never glide to me

What is whispering in your head? Whom do you call your tormentor?
Never has the reddish green of your eyes smouldered so deceitfully
As in your dealings with the weapon-glistening foe

The fear is the burning wool dress—the blue one that I bought for you
It embraces you and keeps you from coming to me
You are burning in its fabric and crying like a wailing bird

YVAN GOLL (1891–1950) was born in Alsace-Lorraine, was bilingual in
French and German, and wrote in both languages at different times of
his life. He worked with the Dadaists in Zürich, with the Expressionists
in Berlin, and with the Surrealists in Paris. His satiric drama *Methusalem,
or the Eternal Bourgeois* (1921), was a precursor to the Theatre of the
Absurd; his 'Manifesto for Surrealism' honoured Apollinaire and debated
Breton; his early interest in film yielded *Chapliniade*. His life as a novelist,
playwright, translator and publisher produced collaborations with Chagall,
Dalí, Picasso, Léger, Weill, Joyce, among others. During his exile years
in New York in the '30s and '40s he published W.C. Williams, Breton,
Patchen, Henry Miller, as well as a collection of his own poems, written
in English, *Fruit from Saturn*. Following the diagnosis of his leukæmia, he
wrote the passionate last poems in the volume *Traumkraut*, from which the
poems here are drawn. Nan Watkins' translation of the book, *Dreamweed*,
will appear from Black Lawrence Press in the USA in 2012.

NAN WATKINS is a writer, translator and musician. She lives in the Blue
Ridge Mountains near Asheville, North Carolina. Her publications in-
clude *East Toward Dawn: A Woman's Solo Journey Around the World*
and *Rare Birds* (University Press of Mississippi), her conversations with
musicians, made together with Thomas Rain Crowe. Her translations from
the German include Karin Struck's *Voluntary Death* (Dimension), and
Christine Brückner's *Sappho's Farewell* (Oxygen). She has also translated
Claire Goll's poems in *10,000 Dawns: The Love Poems of Yvan & Claire
Goll* (White Pine Press) and has published translations of Yvan Goll's
poems in *Asheville Poetry Review, International Poetry Review* and *Beloit
Poetry Journal*.

Notes on Contributors

TIM ALLEN's *Settings* was published by Shearsman in 2008.

RICHARD BERENGARTEN's *Selected Writings,* in five volumes, have been appearing in new editions from Shearsman Books this year.

LINDA BLACK is co-editor of *The Long Poem Magazine,* and author of two Shearsman collections, the most being *Root* (2011).

ANDY BROWN has two collections from Salt: a selected poems, *Flight of the Rebel Angels,* and *Goose Music,* jointly-authored with John Burnside. He teaches Creative Writing at the University of Exeter.

MARIANNE BURTON lives in London. Her chapbook, *The Devil's Cut,* was published by Smith's Knoll in 2007.

ANTHONY CALESHU lives in Plymouth where he teaches at the University. His most recent publication is *On Whales* (Salt, 2010).

KEN COCKBURN is a poet and translator based in Edinburgh. He has translated Thomas Brasch and Thomas Rosenlöcher, among others.

ANAMARÍA CROWE SERRANO lives in Dublin. Translator of a number of Spanish and Italian poets, her own first collection, *Femispheres,* was published by Shearsman Books in 2008.

RACHEL GIPPETTI, originally from the USA, now lives in Plymouth.

MARK GOODWIN has two Shearsman collections, the more recent being *Back of A Vast* (2010); another book, *Shod,* from Nine Arches Press in Rugby, won the 2011 East Midlands Book Award.

GERARD GREENWAY is editor of *Angelaki* and works as a tutor in philosophy and literature at Oxford University.

HARRY GUEST's most recent collection is *Some Times* (Anvil, 2010). His Collected Poems, *A Puzzling Harvest,* is available from the same publisher; his Shearsman collection, *Comparisons & Conversions,* appeared in 2008.

ROSS HAIR teaches at the University of Portsmouth. More of his work is forthcoming from *LVNG* and Skysill Press.

LUCY HAMILTON lives in Cambridge, and is a regular contributor.

BRIAN HENRY has published six books of poetry, most recently *Wings Without Birds* (Salt, 2010). He also have translated Tomaž Šalamun's *Woods and Chalices* (Harcourt, 2008) and Aleš Šteger's *The Book of Things* (BOA Editions, 2010). He has co-edited *Verse* magazine since 1995.

MARY LEADER teaches at Purdue University, Indiana. Her third collection, *Beyond the Fire,* appeared from Shearsman in 2010.

TOM LOWENSTEIN has two Shearsman collections, most recently *Conversation with Murasaki* (2009). The text here is drawn from his next Shearsman volume, due for publication in 2012.

RUPERT LOYDELL is editor of *Stride Magazine*. He has three collections from Shearsman Books, *Wildlife* (2011) being the most recent.

JAMES MCLAUGHLIN lives in Dumbarton. Knives, Forks & Spoons Press (Manchester) published his chapbook, *Aeido*, in 2011.

CHANTAL MAILLARD is a Spanish poet of Belgian origin. The poems here are drawn form the volume *Hilos* (2007). Among her many awards are the Premio Nacional de Poesía, 2004.

CHRISTINE MARENDON is a German poet. She studied Italian in Erlangen and Siena, works as a translator and publicist, and lives in Hamburg.

GEORGE MESSO has two collections of his own work from Shearsman, and has also translated Ilhan Berk, Gonca Özmen and the *Ikinci Yeni* for the press, the last of which has been shortlisted for the Poetry Society's 2011 Popescu Translation prize. His anthology of Turkish women poets, *From This Bridge*, appeared in 2010.

DAVID MILLER lives in London. His book, *The Waters of Marah: Collected Prose* (2005) is available from Shearsman Books, and from Singing Horse Press in the USA. *Spiritual Letters (I–V)* is available from Chax Press.

TARA REBELE lives in the USA, where her book of performance texts, *And I'm Not Jenny*, was published by Slope Editions in 2005.

ELIZABETH ROBINSON has published many books in the USA. Notable recent collections include *Inaudible Trumpeters* (Harbor Mountain Press, 2008) and *Also Known As* (Apogee Press, 2009). She lives in Colorado.

JAIME ROBLES, from California, is currently reading for a PhD at the University of Exeter. *Anime Animus Anima* (2010) is a Shearsman title.

GAVIN SELERIE's *Music's Duel: New and Selected Poems* was published by Shearsman Books in 2009.

ZOË SKOULDING is editor of *Poetry Wales* and has two collections from Seren, *The Mirror Trade* (2004) and *Remains of a Future City* (2010).

STEVE SPENCE's Shearsman collection, *A Curious Shipwreck,* was shortlisted for the 2010 Forward Prize. *Limits of Control* was published in 2011 by Penned in the Margins, London.

JANET SUTHERLAND has two collections from Shearsman Books, the more recent being *Hangman's Acre* (2009).

JOHAN DE WIT lives in London. Publications include *Up to You, Munro* and *No Hand Signals: the invisibility of language in poetry* (both Veer Press).

HYAM YARED is a francophone Lebanese writer, based in Beirut. She has published three poetry collections and two novels. Among several awards, she has received the Prix France-Liban.

For information on Yvan Goll and Nan Watkins, please see page 105.

Lightning Source UK Ltd.
Milton Keynes UK
UKOW051817111011

180175UK00001B/51/P